Experiments with ROCKS

Christine Taylor-Butler

Heinemann
LIBRARY
Chicago, Illinois

www.heinemannraintree.com
Visit our website to find out more information about Heinemann-Raintree books.

To order:
☎ Phone 888-454-2279
💻 Visit www.heinemannraintree.com to browse our catalog and order online.

Edited by Rebecca Rissman, Dan Nunn, and Catherine Veitch
Designed by Richard Parker
Picture research by Tracy Cummins
Originated by Capstone Global Library
Printed in the United States of America
in North Mankato, Minnesota.
052013   007422RP

15 14 13
10 9 8 7 6 5 4 3

Library of Congress Cataloging-in-Publication Data
Taylor-Butler, Christine.
   Experiments with rocks / Christine Taylor-Butler.—1st ed.
      p. cm.—(My science investigations)
   Includes bibliographical references and index.
   ISBN 978-1-4329-5360-7 (hc)—ISBN 978-1-4329-5366-9 (pb) 1. Rocks—Experiments—Juvenile literature. 2. Science projects—Juvenile literature. I. Title.
   QE432.2.T39 2012
   552.0078—dc22   2010042651

Acknowledgments
We would like to thank the following for permission to reproduce photographs: Getty Images p. 28 (Chip Chipman/ Bloomberg); Heinemann Raintree pp. 8, 11, 12, 13, 14, 16, 17, 18, 19, 20, 21, 22, 23, 24, 25, 26, 27 (Karon Dubke); Istockphoto p29 (© bonnie Jacobs); Shutterstock pp. 4 (© Daniel Lohmer), 5 (© Paul B. Moore), 6 (© Claudia Holzmann).

Cover photograph of a boy finding things on a pebble beach reproduced with permission of Corbis (© Ashely Jouhar). Background photograph of brown stone reproduced with permission of Shutterstock (© Merkushev Vasiliy).

Special thanks to Suzy Gazlay for her invaluable help in the preparation of this book. We would also like to thank Ashley Wolinski for her help in the preparation of this book.

Every effort has been made to contact copyright holders of material reproduced in this book. Any omissions will be rectified in subsequent printings if notice is given to the publisher.

Disclaimer
All the Internet addresses (URLs) given in this book were valid at the time of going to press. However, due to the dynamic nature of the Internet, some addresses may have changed, or sites may have changed or ceased to exist since publication. While the author and publisher regret any inconvenience this may cause readers, no responsibility for any such changes can be accepted by either the author or the publisher.

Contents

Some words are printed in bold, **like this.**
You can find out what they mean by looking
in the Glossary.

A Rocky Start

Rocks are all around us. There are small rocks all around. There are large rocks in the mountains. Some people wear rocks as jewelry. There are many different kinds of rocks on our planet.

Scientists who study rocks are called **geologists**.
They find out how rocks are made. This helps
us to learn how Earth was made, and how it is
changing.

How Scientists Work

Scientists start with a question about something they **observe**, or notice. They gather information and think about it. Then they make a guess, or **hypothesis**, about a likely answer to their question. Next they set up an **experiment** to test their hypothesis. They look at the **data**, or **results**, and make a decision, or **conclusion**, about whether their hypothesis is right or wrong.

Scientists experiment with rocks of all sizes.

How To Do an Experiment

1. Start a **log**. Write down your **observations**, question, and hypothesis.
2. Plan step-by-step how you can test the hypothesis. This is called the **procedure**.
3. Carry out the experiment. **Record** everything that happens. These are your observations.
4. Compare your results with your hypothesis. Was your hypothesis right or wrong? What did you learn? The answer is your conclusion.

Observe

↓

Hypothesis

↓

Experiment

↓

Data

↓

Conclusion

↙ ↘

Hypothesis True   Hypothesis False

Properties of Rocks

Rocks have different **properties**, or features. Rocks can be different colors, shapes, **textures**, and sizes. Like **geologists**, we can use properties to **classify**, or sort, rocks into different groups.

Procedure

1. Find ten very different rocks. Draw a chart in your **log** like the one on the opposite page.
2. Choose a rock. Look at it closely with a magnifying glass. Draw a picture of it in your table.

Collect these things for your **experiment**.

3. Fill out the rest of the row: color (as many as you see), texture (rough or smooth), **luster** (shiny or dull), and features (anything you notice, such as sharp edges).
4. Do the same for each rock in your collection.
5. Put your rocks in a pile. Read the properties you have written for one rock. See if a friend can pick out the rock you are describing.

Rock	Picture	Color	Texture	Luster	Features
1.					
2.					
3.					
4.					
5.					

Make a chart like this in your log to **record** your findings.

Learning More

There are three kinds of rock. They are made in different ways.

Igneous Rock

Magma is hot liquid rock deep inside Earth. When magma cools, it becomes **igneous** rock. Some igneous rock are glassy. These rocks contain **crystals**.

Sedimentary Rock

Wind and rain can break up rocks. The pieces mix with shells, plants, and dead animals. Layers pile up on top of another. In time, they become **sedimentary** rocks. These rocks often have layers. You may also be able to see sand, tiny rocks, or pieces of shells in sedimentary rocks.

Metamorphic Rock

Deep inside Earth, high temperatures and pressures change igneous and sedimentary rocks. They become **metamorphic** rocks. Metamorphic rocks may have bands of color or layers of crystals.

Look again at each of your rocks. What kind do you think each rock may be? Why?

Diamond

Diamonds are a kind of igneous rock.

Bubbling Rocks

Limestone is a kind of **sedimentary** rock. It is formed from the shells of billions of tiny sea creatures. Chalk is a kind of limestone.

Vinegar is a weak **acid**. If vinegar is dropped on some kinds of rocks, they bubble. Limestone is one of those rocks. Rocks related to limestone will bubble, too.

Hypothesis

A rock that bubbles when acid is dropped on it is limestone or is related to limestone.

You will need these things for your **experiment**.

Procedure

1. Place a piece of chalk and 10 different rocks in a cake pan. Put two drops of water on the chalk. What happens?

2. Repeat step 1 using vinegar instead of water. **Record** your **observations**.

Watch carefully for any changes in the chalk.

3. Put two drops of vinegar on each rock.
4. Put the rocks that bubble into one pile. Put the rocks that do not bubble into another pile.

The Science Explained

Rocks that contain limestone or are related to limestone will bubble when **acid** is dropped on them.

Rock number	Did it bubble?	Does it contain limestone?
1.		
2.		
3.		
4.		

Make a chart like this in your **log** to **record** your **results**.

Does It Hold Water?

Rocks look solid. But many rocks are not. Most rocks have tiny holes called **pores**. Some rocks have larger pores, or more pores, than others. Are you surprised that some rocks can **absorb**, or take in, water? The water comes in through the pores. Rocks can also hold water in cracks.

Hypothesis

The larger the rock, the more water it can hold.

You will need these things for your **experiment**.

Procedure

1. Place eight different rocks in a shallow bowl.
2. Put one drop of water on the first rock. Add another drop. Does the water roll off? Does it soak in?
3. Repeat step 2 with the other rocks. **Record** your **observations**.

Watch carefully to see what happens when you drop water on the rocks.

4. Line up your rocks in order from smallest to largest. Place each rock in a cup.
5. Pour half a cup of water over each rock. Leave the rocks in the water for one hour.
6. Pour the water from the first cup back into the measuring cup. How much water is left? **Record** your answer in your **log**.
7. Repeat step 6 with the other rocks.
8. Look at your **data**. Did the larger rocks always hold more water than the smaller rocks?

If the rock has **absorbed** water, there will be less than half a cup poured back into the measuring cup.

The Science Explained

The amount of water a rock holds depends on the size and number of **pores** it has. So a larger rock may not hold more water than a smaller one.

Pore

Some pores are easy to see. Others are very small.

Tumbling Rocks

Over time, rocks change size and shape. Wind blows sand into them and wears them down. Water gets into cracks and freezes, causing rocks to break. Rocks in the oceans and rivers hit against each other. The way wind and water change rocks is called **weathering**.

Hypothesis

Moving water causes rocks to bump into each other and break into smaller pieces over time.

You will need these things for this **experiment**.

Procedure

1. Put some rocks in the bottom of a plastic container. Cover the rocks with water, put the lid on, then shake it for five minutes.

2. Take the lid off. Is the water clear or muddy? What happens if you shake the rocks for five more minutes?

When rocks hit each other over and over again, they begin to break down.

Make sure you use a container that is sturdy enough for this activity, so you don't get wet!

21

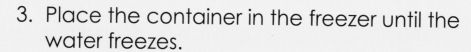

3. Place the container in the freezer until the water freezes.
4. Has anything happened to the rocks?
5. Let the water melt and then put the container back into the freezer. Repeat this four times. **Record** your **observations**.

Use your **log** to write down any changes you see.

The Science Explained

Water gets into the **pores** in rock. Water expands, or takes up more space, when it freezes. It shrinks when it melts. Over time, this can break up rocks. **Weathering** can wear away part of a mountain.

Did any of your rocks break in the freezer?

23

Crystals Rock!

All rocks are made of **minerals**. Some are made of just one mineral, and some are made of many. Most minerals are found naturally as **crystals.** Crystals aren't alive, but they can grow by sticking to other crystals of the same kind.

Hypothesis

Crystals will grow more quickly in the fridge than they will at room temperature.

You will need these things for your **experiment**.

Procedure

1. Measure 1/4 cup of Epsom salts into a bowl.

2. Pour 1/4 cup of hot tap water over the Epsom salts. Add two drops of food coloring. Stir until most of the Epsom salts have **dissolved**.

3. Place the bowl in a fridge for two hours. What do you see? Leave it for another two hours. Has anything changed? **Record** your **observations**.

4. Repeat steps 1 and 2 using another bowl. Put the bowl on a table or shelf in the room for two hours. What do you see? Leave it for another two hours. How is it different from the bowl in the fridge?

Warning!

Do not drink or eat the crystals. Epsom salts are not the same as the salt we put on food.

Make a Model Geode

Have you ever seen a **geode**? It's a rock with **crystals** on the inside. You can make a model of a geode in this **experiment**.

You will need these things for your experiment.

Procedure

1. Add salt to hot water in a bowl one spoonful at a time, stirring gently, until it stops **dissolving**. Add two drops of food coloring.

2. Crack an egg in half. Empty and clean the shell. Place one half of the shell in a cup. Fill the shell with your colored salt water. Place the cup on a sunny window ledge.

3. Check your experiment every day. **Record** your **observations**. What happens once all the liquid has disappeared?

Some geodes take thousands of years to form. How long did your model take?

Your Turn!

The rocks in your local area might be millions of years old. A **geologist** can tell a lot about a rock by its appearance and where it is found. Geologists use what they know about rocks to help design bridges, dams, and tunnels.

You've learned a lot about rocks! What else would you like to know? How could you find out? Think of a way to design an **experiment** that would help answer your question.

Glossary

absorb suck up, or take in

acid chemical that can dissolve some materials

classify group things that have similar properties

conclusion what you learn from the results of an experiment

crystal form of mineral with a very regular structure

data information gathered in an experiment

dissolve melt in a liquid

experiment organized way of testing an idea

geode hollow rock filled with crystals

geologist scientist who studies rocks and soil

hypothesis suggested statement or explanation that can be tested

igneous kind of rock formed from cooling magma

log written notes about an experiment

luster how a rock or mineral looks when light shines on it

magma rock that has been melted by high temperatures

metamorphic kind of rock formed under heat and pressure

mineral substance found in the ground that makes up rocks

observation something that you notice using any of your five senses

observe watch, or notice, something

pores small holes in a rock or other solid object

procedure steps followed to carry out an experiment

properties traits or characteristics that can be observed or measured

record draw or write something down

results what happens in an experiment

sedimentary kind of rock formed from layers of other materials

texture how something feels when you touch it. For example, smooth or rough.

weathering process of breaking rock into soil, sand, and other small pieces

Find Out More

Books

Lindeen, Carol K. *Rock Basics*. Mankato, Minn.: Capstone, 2008.

Mayer, Cassie. *Rocks*. Chicago: Heinemann, 2008.

Tomecek, Steve. *Jump Into Science: Rocks and Minerals*. Washington, D.C.: National Geographic, 2010.

Websites

American Museum Of Natural History
www.amnh.org/ology/index.php?channel=earth

The Field Museum (Chicago) Virtual Tour
www.fieldmuseum.org/
undergroundadventure/virtual_tour/index.shtml

Wonderville—Discover the fun of science
www.wonderville.ca/browse/activities

Index